Widower's

by
Terry Harper

The play was originally produced by The Bijou Theatre Club, at the Palace Avenue Theatre. Paignton, Devon on December 4th, 5th & 6th 1997 with the following cast:-Directed by Jill Farrant.

Peter Mason . . . . **Alan Tanner**

Rosie Mason . . . . **Lora Grochala**

Gerald . . . . **Mark Saturley**

Jenny . . . . **Lyn Wilson**

Christine Mason . . . . **Isobel Goss**

Colin . . . . **David Hyde-Constantine**

Susan . . . . **Yvonne Dawe**

Characters
The Mason Family

Peter Mason
Rosie Mason
Gerald . . . . *their son*
Jenny . . . . *their daughter*
Christine Mason . . . . *Peter's mother*
Colin . . . . *Jenny's partner*
Susan . . . . *Gerald's wife*

Friends
Fiona . . . . . Dr Reynolds . . . . Anne

Acquaintances
Louisa . . . . . Mandy

Strangers
Evangelist . . . . . Woman in pub . . . . . Woman in pub

ACT I

Before the curtain rises we hear Glyn Kerslake's original song "The Smile you left behind". This continues as the curtain rises on an unlit stage then lights come slowly up on Peter Mason, seated centre stage rear. This area is a rostrum and is approached by two steps to the front and two steps to the stage left side. He remains motionless. Lights up on his son Gerald and his daughter-in-law Susan. Downstage left from Gerald and Susan is Granny. Light up on her. Downstage left of Granny is Mandy, the flower-shop proprietor, she is holding a gift wrapped display of flowers and against the proscenium there stands a floral display unit. Light this. Rear stage right light Peter's daughter Jenny, and her boy-friend Colin. Slightly downstage from them stands the evangelist, and downstage again from him stands Louisa the pub landlady and seated on a stool at table is Anne Dyson. Light this. At the director's discretion the music fades, and spotlight downstage right against the proscenium arch on Rosie, Peter's dead wife.

ROSIE: Poor old Peter... he desperately wants the phone to ring... wants someone to call him if they don't, he'll phone someone, just to talk to them. *(Peter stands up and moves hesitatingly to telephone on sideboard behind his chair)* No, wait a minute, he won't do that today, he's fighting it. He's done it before, and it didn't work, because whoever he phoned didn't know what to say... or had other things on their minds. Things which he didn't know about, things which didn't matter to him, but which mattered to them, and which at the time he phoned mattered more to them than he did... I wonder if he's learnt that yet? *(Moves towards rostrum)* If only I could get through to him. It's tough Peter, tough as hell... but there is a way... it's just up to you to find it.

PETER: *(Telephone rings. He smiles and lifts receiver)* Hello, Peter Mason speaking... *(He listens and the smile drops)* No... no I do not want a fitted kitchen. *(Slams receiver down and moves to his chair. Sits. Picks up photograph of Rosie from table and looks at it as she moves to upstage right of him on rostrum)* Saturday October 22nd. We'd have been married thirty years today... if you'd still been alive. Oh God! I wish you could speak to me, Rosie. *(Puts photograph back on table)*

ROSIE: I can speak to you, it's just that you can't hear me. You're on another planet. *(Moves in closer to Peter)* Then you often were.

PETER: It was a bright autumn morning.

ROSIE: It was a dull and overcast... just like him.

PETER: I'd have thought the kids would have remembered.

ROSIE: They probably don't know what to say. They might even think it'll upset him if they do ring.

PETER: Perhaps they think it'll upset me.

ROSIE: Here... I wonder if he can hear me?

PETER: I wouldn't mind being upset. It's better than being ignored. They could bloody well phone.

ROSIE: Why doesn't he phone them. He's become so insular since I died.

PETER: I suppose I could give them a ring. No, damn it, why should I? *(Stands up)* If they can';t be bothered on a special day like this. Right! *(Moves to steps off rostrum)* I'm going to have a shampoo, shave and a... bath. *(Moves offstage left. Rosie moves offstage right. Lights up on Jenny and Colin. He is at desk typing. She is on telephone.)*

COLIN: Who are you phoning?

JENNY: Daddy. You know what day it is?

COLIN: Saturday.

JENNY: His first wedding anniversary without Mum. The numbers engaged.

COLIN: You'd better try again later.

(Fade lights on Jenny and Colin. Bring up lights on Gerald and Susan. Gerald has a mobile telephone and paces with it. Bring up lights on rostrum. We hear Peter's telephone ringing. It continues to ring through Gerald's conversation with Susan.)

GERALD: I can't understand it. Why isn't Dad at home? He never goes to the office on Saturday's

SUSAN: Look Gerald, he's on his own now. He's probably out shopping. He's got to do everything for himself you know.

GERALD: He knows Jenny and I always ring him n his wedding anniversary. *(Puts telephone down. Peter's telephone stops ringing. Cut lights on Gerald*

and Susan and on rostrum. Lights up on Jenny and Colin. Jenny is on the telephone. Colin at typewriter.)

COLIN: Trying Peter again? Bit soon isn't it?

JENNY: No, I'm trying Granny to see if she's been in touch. *(Speaks into telephone)* Oh, hello Granny, it's Jenny

(Lights up on Granny sitting in armchair speaking on telephone both scenes are now lit.)

GRANNY: Jenny, how nice to hear from you.

JENNY: Have you been in touch with Daddy?

GRANNY: No.

JENNY: It's his wedding anniversary and I haven't been able to get through. The phone is either engaged or not answering.

GRANNY: At the moment sweetheart your father is hurting. He's probably phoning anybody just to talk to someone. I bet he's free-phoning car insurance and double glazing. He calls it prospective clients revenge.

JENNY: You will phone him sometime, won't you Granny?

GRANNY: Of course I will. I am his mother. I don't know what'll come of it, because I don't know what I'm going to say to him, but I'll ring him.

(Fade lights on Granny and Jenny. Lights up on rostrum. Peter enters from stage left putting on his wrist watch)

PETER: Is that all the time is? God, today's never going to end. It's only a quarter to eleven in the morning now. *(Sits in chair)* I keep remembering those lines from that play 'Pack of Lies'... "I miss her more, not less, is it always like that?"

ROSIE: *(Upstage of Peter)* Any minute now he's going to tell my photograph that he misses me terribly. Then he'll have a drink, and neither will do him any good, but he thinks they will. He always thought a drink would do him good. Nearly cost him his job before he pulled himself together.

PETER: *(Standing up. Picks up Rosie's photograph)* I miss you terribly.

ROSIE: If predictability was a fiver he'd be very well off. It's a pity, but he's going to get worse before he gets better today. *(Moves off rostrum and exits right)*

PETER:(*Pours himself a whisky. Salutes Rosie's photograph*) To my wedding anniversary... our wedding anniversary. Love you, darling. (*Drinks a toast. Door bell rings Peter comes down steps from rostrum moves right. The evangelist enters carrying a Bible in downstage hand*)

EVANGELIST: Good morning my friend. Tell me, have you found Jesus?

PETER: Jesus who?

EVANGELIST: Tell me, are you an atheist?

PETER: God knows. (*Holds up hand for the man to stay where he is*) That's far enough. Are you selling something?

EVANGELIST: Heaven forbid.

PETER: Because you might as well know straight away that I am not in the market for on the knocker negotiations.

EVANGELIST: Far from selling my friend... I am bringing you the word of God.

PETER: (*Getting annoyed*) Let me tell you something about God. He wasn't round when I needed him. He took my Rosie... (*Snaps his fingers*) just like that. One second she was here, and the next... she was gone. (*Backs man offstage right*) Go away... and when you're getting your next set of words from God, you can tell him I don't think much of him. (*Man exits. Peter returns to rostrum and sits*)

ROSIE: (*in spotlight stage R*) Tolerance was never his strong point.

PETER: (*Looks at watch again then at telephone*) Right that's it. Nobody is going to ring. Thoughtless sods. What the hell do we have children for? They must know what I'm feeling like. (*Gets up*) I'll take those flowers down to Rosie. (*Exits stage left*)

ROSIE: Poor old Peter. He never expected to be the one who was left... I suppose nobody ever does.

(*Fade lights on Rosie. Lights up on Granny. She is standing by her telephone*)

GRANNY: Now what on earth am I going to say? Happy anniversary Peter is completely inappropriate. How are you Peter? (*Presses buttons on her telephone. Telephone on rostrum begins to ring*) That's better... bit negative, but better. Peter, I've been thinking about you... no, no, no, that's no good. Have you heard from Jenny? No blast it, I know he hasn't. I didn't know it was going to be this difficult. *(Deep breath)* Peter, I've been thinking, why don't you... why doesn't he what? Ah! Wait a minute... Peter, I saw Mabel the other day, she was asking after you... that's no good, he can't stand her... oh dear.

(Peter enters stage left carrying a bunch of flowers. Moves to telephone. Cut lights on Granny. His telephone stops ringing.)

PETER: Would you believe it. Some people have no patience. *(Turns and exits left. Cut lights on rostrum. Lights up on pub downstage right. Two women are seated on stools upstage and to the right of the table and two stools which are the focal point. Louisa the landlady picks up an empty glass from the table. Moves up to the two women. Mimes a short conversation. Peter carrying the flowers enters stage left and crosses to pub area. Sits at table on which he puts flowers. Takes out a card and starts to write. An attractive woman, mid forties enters stage left. Takes off her raincoat and shakes it. Crosses to table and looks at Peter as he is writing. Frowns slightly.)*

ANNE: Peter... Peter Mason?

PETER: *(Standing up)* Eh... good morning... yes... I';m afraid I don't...

ANNE: You can't remember me, can you?

PETER: Your face is familiar, but I...

(The two women exchange glances.)

ANNE: Do you remember Tony Dyson?

PETER: Tony Dyson... Tony Dyson... yes, of course, medium paced out swing bowler.

ANNE: Oh, is that what he did?

PETER: Yes. If there was a cross wind from say long on, he could be quite devastating. You... you're not Anne Dyson?

ANNE: The ex-Anne Dyson. Divorced nearly three years now.

(The two women react to this statement)

PETER: Oh... oh dear... I'm sorry... eh... won't you sit down? Will you have a drink?

ANNE: Thank you. *(Sits)* Gin and tonic please.

PETER: *(Sitting)* Louisa, Gin and tonic, and a whisky for me, please.

LOUISA: Right Peter. *(Leaves two women and exits)*

PETER: Was it still raining when you came in?

ANNE: Absolutely tipping it down, that's why I came in here.

PETER: How long since you've been in these parts then?

ANNE: Oh, let me see... must be five or six years I should think... yes, it must be.

PETER: So what are you doing with yourself, workwise I mean.

ANNE: I got a job in PR for a hotel chain after the divorce. I've been in America.

PETER: Pretty exciting by the sound of it.

LOUISA: *(Puts Gin and tonic and whisky on table. Peter pays her)* Thank's Peter. *(Smiles at Anne. Exits)*

ANNE: *(Takes a drink)* Cheers! Pardon me for saying so, but those are lovely flowers.

PETER: Yes... they're for Rosie.

ANNE: *(Warm smile)* Rosie... ah yes, we used to have lots of laughs in the old days. How is she?

PETER: She died just over a year ago.

ANNE: Oh my God! How terrible. Oh Peter... I feel dreadful... what can I say?

PETER: It's all right. You didn't know, how could you have done? Don't worry, it's more embarrassing for you than me. I've got used to it... well... I'm getting used to it... used to coping with it anyhow... in the end that's what it boils down to.

ANNE: I'm so very sorry... I've no idea what to say. I feel completely useless.

PETER: *(Drinks)* You mustn't. There's no point in upsetting yourself. It happened, and that's it.

ANNE: Do you ant to talk about it... or...?

PETER: *(Shrugs and indicates flowers)* I was taking these flowers to Rosie when it started to pour, so I came in here.

(The two women get up and cross behind Peter and Anne towards stage left. They look back at Peter and Anne)

ANNE: Peter...

PETER:... Yes?

ANNE: Could I come with you? I'd like to pay my last respects... that's if you don't mind.

PETER: What a nice thought. Rosie'd like that. We'll go when it stops raining.

(The two women look at each other then exit)

ANNE:*(Picks up card Peter has been writing)* "To my darling Rosie... just round the corner. All my love, Peter" That's beautiful... "Jus around the corner".

PETER: It's an improvement on R.I.P. *(Drinks)* It's our thirtieth wedding anniversary today. She isn't really in the grave you know.

ANNE: No?

PETER: No... she's everywhere... the grave is just a token. I talk to her everyday.

ANNE:*(Very gently puts hand on Peter's arm)* How lovely. Must be comforting for you. What do you talk about.

(Rosie enters and stands upstage of table)

ROSIE: He usually tells me that the property market is depressed, and so is he.

PETER: I don't really know. Anything that comes to mind. One thing I can tell you, it doesn't always make sense.

ANNE: Peter... how did it happen? Sorry... you don't have to talk about it if you don't want to.

ROSIE: He's getting better at this bit. Been working on it... giving it a bit of polish. Oh dear, oh dear, I do wish he wouldn't assume the look of a bladder wracked bloodhound. It would never surprise me if he cocked his leg against the table.

PETER: She woke up one morning and said she wasn't feeling very well, went to the bathroom and just dropped down.

ANNE: How awful.

PETER: After a while... perhaps in retrospect you come to realise that it was for the best. I mean... no, not for the best... what I'm trying to say is... she didn't suffer.

ROSIE: How does he know?

PETER: It was quick. She wasn't bedridden, she didn't have some terrible wasting disease, nothing like that.

ANNE: What a shock for you though. I'd have gone mad.

PETER: You're given something, believe me. I don't know what it is... a kind of inner strength... I felt, well, not exactly numb, but sort of detached from life.

ANNE: Didn't you feel angry? I'd have been raving.

PETER: No, that's the strange thing. I think I wanted to be angry with someone or something... God perhaps? I don't know... but I was in a state of unreality. Do you know, I used to have feelings of guilt that I didn't feel sadder about my loss... guilty that I wasn't missing her more. I was outside looking in on life. I do get angry with God now... oh yes. *(Shrugs)* People are very kind you know, Anne.

ROSIE: He's still terrific with a cliche. Any minute now he's going to trot out the one about 'you find your real friends when you're down'.

PETER: I realise that everyone has their own life to get on with. You have to accept that don't you? But you do tend to find out who your real friends are when you're down. And of course, there's the family.

(Cut lights on Peter and Anne and Rosie. Bring up lights on Jenny and Colin)

COLIN: Do you think Peter will mind being proxy God-father, Jen?

JENNY: *(Putting receiver back on telephone)* I'll let you know if I ever get through to him. I've been trying on and off since half past nine, now it's nearly one. Where's he got to?

COLIN: Down the pub if he's any sense.

JENNY: You don't think anything has happened to him, do you?

COLIN: Such as?

JENNY: Well, he's a dear soul and all that, but you know how useless he is round the house. He might have tried to mend something and had an accident.

COLIN: Not a chance. *(Stands up)* If Peter wanted something mended he'd have got somebody to do it. *(Puts arm round her shoulders)* Now don't start panicking. He's going through a rough time, I understand that, but... well in every marriage one partner is going to go before the other. That's not sod's law, that's God's law.

JENNY: Thanks Colin. I do worry about him, but he does get on my nerves at times.

COLIN:*(Sitting at desk)* Try him again later... and Jen... I think he'd like to know you worry about him.

(Fade lights on Jenny and Colin. Lights up again on Peter and Anne in the pub)

ANNE:*(Taking a drink)* Will you come round and have dinner with me tonight? I'm staying at the Royal Sovereign until tomorrow. I have to be in London in the afternoon.

PETER: Eh... well...

ROSIE:... God, if you're not doing anything important at the moment, give him a boot up the backside. He'll blow it if he's left on his own.

ANNE: I'm sure Rosie wouldn't mind.

PETER: No... no of course she wouldn't. It's just that... well... being my... eh our anniversary... I thought I'd stay at home.

ROSIE: And have a riotous time re-reading his sympathy cards.

ANNE: And mope? Is that what you really want to do? I don't doubt for a minute that it's been as rough as hell for you Peter... but living in the past isn't the answer.

PETER: Everyone says that... everyone that hasn't been there that is. A wise man once said everyone can accept grief, providing it's someone else's.

ANNE: Sorry. I wasn't being fair.

ROSIE: Don't give into him Anne. I made that mistake too many times when we were married. He had a habit of standing there like a lost schoolboy when he didn't get his own way... just like he's looking now. Come on Anne, give it your best shot.

ANNE:*(As Peter gives her a hand to put on her raincoat)* You know it's not very flattering for a girl to have her invitation turned down.

PETER: Oh but... oh no... I didn't mean... oh good heavens, no, no, you've got it all wrong. It isn't that I don't appreciate your invitation.

ANNE: But you don't think you ought to accept it.

ROSIE: Now he's really confused.

PETER: No, that isn't true. I can please myself. I don't have anyone else to consider, do I?

ANNE:I just thought it might be a bit more fun than eating on your own... being on your own for that matter. *(Smiles sympathetically)* I think I understand, Peter... you must have loved her very much.

PETER:I did. And because I did, I'd love to come to dinner with you tonight. I'm not really much of a cook, but even that's better than going out to eat on your own. I've never known such a lonely place as a crowded restaurant, when you're there on your own. *(Picks up flowers and moves to Anne)* You're right, I would have sat at home and moped. And it wouldn't have done any good. It never does. *(Peter and Anne exit)*

ROSIE: Thank's God. You can go back to doing whatever it was you were doing, and give yourself some Brownie points. You've got him going out to dinner. *(Looks across to where Peter and Anne exited)* Thank's Anne. *(Rosie exits right. Cut lights on pub. Lights up on Jenny who is speaking on telephone)*

JENNY:*(As lights come up on rostrum. Peter on telephone)* Daddy... oh thank goodness, you're there at last. I've been trying to get through all morning. Where have you been?

PETER: Hello Jenny. I've been... oh round and about... have you phoned because it's...

JENNY:... Of course. We always ring on your wedding anniversary.

PETER: Yes I know... but... well... Mum's not here now you know.

JENNY: I bet she is. She loved her wedding anniversaries. She's there, it's just that you can't see her, and she can't speak to you.

PETER: That's a nice thought. Perhaps you're right. I don't know.

JENNY: Of course I'm right. How are you?

PETER: Oh I'm... *(Big effort)* fine. How are you and eh...

JENNY: *(Uptight)*... Colin... it's still Colin, daddy.

PETER: Oh... oh yes. All right is he?

JENNY: Only terrific.

ROSIE:*(On rostrum downstage from Peter)* All because Jenny and Colin aren't married. One of Peter's main faults is that at times he thinks he's a born again Puritan.

JENNY: The baby's doing well.

PETER: Oh... that's... that's nice.

ROSIE: His only grandson, and morally he classifies him as a bastard.

JENNY: Oh Daddy... there was something Colin and I wanted to ask you.

PETER: What is it?

JENNY: It's about the Christening Sunday week.

PETER: Eh... yes?

JENNY: Would you stand as proxy God-Father? Slade Dorval, a friend of Colin's who was going to be God-Father can't make it... he's doing a recording session. He was on Top-of-the-Pops last week.

PETER: Oh dear... I must have missed it. Proxy God-Father?

JENNY: That's right, and Daddy, will you pick up Granny on the way. It'll save her a taxi.

PETER: Is Mother going to the Christening?

JENNY: Of course she is. She is family.

PETER: Which is more than can be said for...

JENNY:... For goodness sake Daddy, don't go on and on about Colin and I not being married. The Priest doesn't object, and I am an ex-virgin of this parish. Got to fly, time for baby's feed. See you at the Christening. Bye. *(Puts telephone down)* Oh he's such a plonker at times. Why can't he live in today. *(Exits right. Cut lights on Jenny)*

PETER:(*Puts telephone down and sits in chair. Looks at photograph of Rosie*)
I know nothing stays the same for ever, but surely there ought to be some
fixed standards. I don't want to go. Isn't that awful? I don't want to go to my
own grandson's Christening. It won't be the same without you, Rosie. I do love
Jenny, you know that, but I can't take itColin... it's no good, I've tried. I
suppose we live in different worlds. I could cope if you were with me, Rosie.
You'd have bridged the gap.

ROSIE: Which makes me sound like a chocolate snack bar. (*Exit left*)

PETER: What's life about anyway? Few weeks fawning sympathy... then... right!
Your course of anti-grief, anti-biotics has been completed, you are now
immune. What were those words of Byron's... ah yes... 'What is the worst of
woes that wait an age? What stamps the wrinkle deeper on the brow? To view
each loved one blotted from the page, and be alone on Earth as I am now'.
(*Shakes head*) I'm being Goddamn selfish. (*Looks at watch*) Should I take
Anne some flowers? Or will it look as if I... what the hell does it matter what
it looks like. (*Gets up goes to telephone*) I'll phone through an order. At least
it's a nice gesture. (*Picks up telephone. Fade lights on rostrum. Lights up
down stage left on floral display. Mandy is arranging one or two blooms*)

MANDY: Typical, isn't it? Hardly a thing all the afternoon, and now Mr Mason
rings in an order just as we're shutting. Still you've got to make allowances for
him I suppose. (*Peter enters*) Evening Mr Mason. Susan is just finishing your
order.

PETER: Thank you, Mandy.

MANDY: You all right, Mr Mason?

PETER: Yes... well you know.

MANDY: Mrs Rollins died this afternoon. We'll be busy on Monday, you mark
my words. I mean, well, you know how it is.

PETER: I know how it is, Mandy.

MANDY: Mind you, she had been lingering. Happy release you might say. Of
course her husband will miss her... bound to. I always think it must be worse
for the husband if the wife goes first. Well, men are a bit helpless on their
own, aren't they? Mine is... can't boil an egg... well he can, but I don't care for

hard boiled eggs, and neither does he. He reckons they bind him up.

PETER: Do they really? Look Mandy, do you think I could have the flowers please, I'm in a bit of a hurry.

MANDY: Of course you can, Mr Mason. Susan is gift wrapping them. You wanted them gift wrapped, didn't you? You said on the phone you wanted them gift wrapped.

PETER: Yes, I wanted them gift wrapped, thank you.

MANDY: Funny thing flowers. I bet none of the people who'll be sending flowers to Mrs Rollins now she's dead, ever sent her any when she was alive and could have appreciated them. Mr Rollins never did, well if he did he never bought them here. The trouble is we don't appreciate people when they're living. You have to die to be really popular. You never hear people say 'oh! She was a rotten old cow!' Oh no, they go all po-faced and say 'There was a lot of good in her you know'.

PETER: Mandy, please may I have the flowers?

MANDY: Yes, yes, Mr Mason. Susan's only got one pair of hands you know. My husband's the same.

PETER: Most people only have one pair of hands.

MANDY:*(Laughing)* Nice one, Mr Mason. No, I meant he hasn't much patience. Men haven't not as a general rule. I mean, have you ever seen them out shopping?

PETER: I'm out shopping, Mandy.

MANDY: Just goes to prove my point then, doesn't it? Have you ever seen a man in the check-out at a supermarket? Caw! St Vitus would never dance again if he could see them. I'll get your flowers. *(Moves off left)* Oh thank you Susan, they're lovely. You've really got a flare for it, you have. *(Enters with gift wrapped flowers)* There you go, Mr Mason.

PETER: Thank you, Mandy. Send the account to the office will you? *(Moves to exit)*

MANDY: Yes, of course. Nice to have a little chat with you. That's what's wrong with people these days, not enough time for a chat... a chat is therapeutic, takes your mind off your troubles. I mean, well, you've had your share, haven't you?

PETER: Yes.

MANDY: But you enjoy a chat, don't you?

PETER: *(Edging away)* Yes.

MANDY: Good. Well I can't stop chatting to you any longer, Mr Mason. It's time to shut the shop.

PETER: Right. Thank you Mandy. *(Exits)*

MANDY: Don't fancy he's looking too well. Bit peaky. Typical man, my husbands the same, especially since he got the last Council Tax bill. *(Exits. As Mandy is saying the above. Backstage crew bring on a table and two chairs. Set it centre stage. On it pot of coffee two cups and saucers, two brandy glasses. Backstage leave. Anne enters stage right. Lights on Anne.)*

ANNE: I wonder how he really feels? I don't suppose he'll tell me... that's even if he knows himself. He must be confused about things... for some of the time at least he must live in the past. I know I did for a while, and I was only divorced.

(Lights up on table. Peter enters stage left. Anne moves and sits at table. Peter sits opposite)

PETER:	Eh...
ANNE:	I...

PETER:	Sorry I...
ANNE:	It's all...

PETER:	Anne...
ANNE:	Peter...

ANNE: Peter, please go ahead or we'll be here all night and say nothing.

PETER: I don't know what I was going to say. It's all gone.

ANNE: *(Very deliberately)* I know you and I never really knew each other very well Peter, but Rosie, she really impressed me. She was one of the most genuine people I ever met. You didn't really care for me when Tony and I lived here, did you? *(Peter is about to deny this)* No, no, don't bother to deny it. You thought I was... oh, I don't know... forward, pushy, a bit man mad.

PETER: You've already said we didn't know each other very well.

ANNE: But you met me as many times as Rosie did, but because she was Rosie, she was, interested in me for what I was, and for no other reason.

PETER: It was just my nature. I don't take to people very quickly... not as a general rule. I mean we only really met because Tony and I played cricket together. If I remember rightly you knew less about the game than Rosie did.

ANNE: There was a big difference. Rosie actually shared your love of the game. I only went along because I needed Tony in those days. She believed in you, Peter.

PETER: *(Taking a drink)* Does this have any relevance, Anne?

ANNE: It has a great deal of relevance for me. Until this morning, I assumed, quite naturally, that Rosie was still alive. It got to me, Peter even though I hadn't seen her for years. You must have been to hell and back.

(Rosie enters stage right and stands upstage of Peter)

PETER: It wasn't very pleasant. *(Pause)* It was awful Anne... it still is. I don't honestly know what life is about. I used to... there was a pattern to it... there was something very well worth having... now there isn't.

ANNE: How do you cope?

PETER: Cope?

ANNE: Sexually.

PETER: You don't beat around the bush, do you?

ANNE: I've never seen the point. I wasn't inviting you to sleep with me.

PETER: I beg your pardon?

ANNE: Don't you miss the physical side of things?

PETER: I... it's... I'll tell you what I miss most. I miss the quiet, gentle, meaningful cuddles. I miss someone to just hold my hand... to me that's not sex... that's love. I think at this particular point in time I'm frightened of a physical relationship.

ROSIE: Poor old Peter... he hasn't changed... thirty years ago tonight he wasn't very good at it either.

ANNE: It's all right Peter. I just thought that it might be a bit of help if you had a frank talk with someone who isn't close to you. Sometimes it's easier that way. *(Puts hand lightly on his arm)* It's too soon... is that it?

PETER: It shouldn't be I suppose, but it is for me.

ROSIE: I know the honeymoon wasn't exactly the Last Tango in Paris... but there were times, many times... then his hormones went on the blink.

PETER: There's a man I know, his wife died about three months before Rosie, and he re-married within a year, and he's ten years older than me.

ANNE: Wanted to get there before the spirit stopped being willing I expect.

PETER: I couldn't do what he did.

ANNE: Couldn't, or wouldn't?

PETER: I don't understand.

ANNE: Is something stopping you letting go of the past?

PETER: No, of course there isn't. It's just that... oh, I don't know what it is. *(Pause)* Yes I do... I still love her, and that's the truth.

ANNE: And you're not ready, not even for a casual affair.

PETER: The situation has never cropped up. *(Smiles)* Of course there are always the Val Malkin's of this world.

ANNE: Who on earth is Val Malkin?

PETER: An old acquaintance of Rosie's and mine. She's a sort of professional virgin, though to hear her talk you'd think she brought the original four and twenty down from Inverness. *(Pause)* Anne, could we change the subject?

ANNE: Of course. I've been a bit intense haven't I? You'll have to excuse me, but then I am a woman.

PETER: You're definitely that.

ROSIE: Coming from him, that's not a bad line of chat.

PETER: *(Standing up)* Well, I've just had a very pleasant evening, Anne, but I must be on my way... eh Gerald... my son, he'll probably phone about eleven, because it's...

ANNE: ... I know what it is, Peter. I do understand.

PETER: When are you leaving?

ANNE: Tomorrow, mid morning.

PETER: *(Holding out his hand. Anne rises and shakes hands)* Oh yes... then I don't suppose we shall...

ANNE: Probably not.

PETER: No... well goodbye Anne. *(She quickly kisses him on the cheek)* Thank you... goodbye. *(He turns away and quickly exits stage left)*

ANNE: Poor lonely bastard. *(She exits slowly stage right as light fades on table scene. Backstage strike table and chairs. Lights up on Gerald. He is on mobile phone. Lights up on rostrum. Peter's telephone starts to ring. Peter enters and picks up telephone)*

PETER: Hello, Peter Mason speaking...

GERALD:... Father, where in God's name have you been all day? I've been trying to get you on and off since early this morning. You know what day it is?

PETER: Oh yes Gerald. *(Looks at Rosie's photograph)* I know what day it is. Is that why you've phoned?

GERALD: Of course it is. We always phone on your anniversary.

PETER: Yes... yes that's right... so you do... Jenny rang earlier.

(Susan enters and stands beside Gerald)

GERALD: *(To Susan)* He sounds a bit shaky to me.

SUSAN: It can't be easy for him.

GERALD: *(Into telephone)* Are you all right, father?

PETER: Yes. I'm... no... I'm feeling pretty low.

GERALD: *(To Susan)* He says he's feeling low.

SUSAN: Give me the phone. *(Takes it from Gerald)* Hello Peter, Susan here. Happy Anniversary.

PETER: Oh Susan.

SUSAN: It's all right Peter. I meant it. Rosie would understand. Think about it... keep your chin up.

PETER: Rosie'd understand?

SUSAN: You know she would. *(Pause)* Peter...

PETER: Yes?

SUSAN: Have a bloody good cry. I'll ring you tomorrow. Goodbye. *(Puts telephone down)*

GERALD: Hey! I haven't finished talking to father.

SUSAN: He doesn't need it tonight, Gerald.

GERALD: What's the matter with him?

SUSAN: Good old fashioned grief. He's got to come out of this bit on his own. I wanted to be sloppy and kind to him, but it would have been wrong.

GERALD: Would it?

SUSAN: Tell me it would have been.

GERALD: *(Embraces her as she starts to cry)* It would have been.

(Cut lights on Gerald and Susan. Keep lights on Peter. He puts telephone down and sits in chair with photograph)

PETER: Why? *(Starts to cry)*

ROSIE: *(To the right of Peter on rostrum)* Oh Peter... what are we going to do with you? More to the point, what are we going to do to you?

PETER: *(Getting control of himself)* Oh dear... I could do with a holiday. It's all getting me down... same bloody routine every day and nobody here when I get home. Where can I go? I could ring Gerald or Jenny tomorrow, one of them would have me. *(Gets up)* Yes, that's what I'll do. *(Puts photo on table)* No... it's not fair on them.

ROSIE: Oh Lord, he's going to do his noble bit now... just when he was beginning to sound positive.

PETER: They don't want an old fool like me mooching round the place. Jenny's got the baby to look after now, and Gerald and Susan are both out at work all day, so I'd be on my own in any case. Might just as well stay where I am.

(Fade lights on Peter. Lights up on Jenny and Colin. Colin is typing. Jenny looks over his shoulder)

JENNY: Are you looking forward to the Christening?

COLIN: I'd be happier if we had a real God-Father. Did Peter actually say he'd stand in?

JENNY: Well... I'm not a hundred per cent sure.

COLIN: What do you mean? Jenny love, the Christening is this Sunday.

JENNY: He sounded sort of bemused the last time I spoke to him.

COLIN: That's about par for the course. *(Grins)* Still Granny will sort him out.

JENNY: That's for sure. Anyhow, just to be on the safe side, I'll give Daddy another ring when he's back from the office tonight. Isn't it strange... I'm sure he hasn't been himself lately. Quite frankly I think he was much better immediately after Mummy died than he is now.

COLIN: Shock coming out I expect. I read somewhere once that it can take anything up to five years to leave your body. It's bound to have an effect.

JENNY: Yes... yes of course. How's the novel coming on? *(Looks over his shoulder as lights fade on Jenny and Colin. Lights up on Granny's flat. Granny is seated in one of the easy chairs. On small table behind the two chairs is a bottle of whisky and two or three glasses. Granny is forthwright in her manner and smartly dressed. Doorbell rings.)*

GRANNY: Is that you, Peter?

PETER: *(Offstage)* Yes.

GRANNY: Door's unlocked. Let yourself in and drop the catch.

PETER: *(Offstage)* Righto!

(Sound of door opening and shutting. Peter enters and puts holdall beside table)

GRANNY: You're early.

PETER: Yes. Easier trip than I expected. The traffic was surprisingly light.

GRANNY: *(Standing up)* Well, come on, give your mother a kiss.

PETER: Mother, really...

GRANNY:... don't be so stuffy Peter. *(Kisses him warmly)* Oh, before I forget, are you staying here tomorrow night after the Christening?

PETER: If it's convenient. It's not very busy at the office, property still isn't moving that quickly, so there's no need to rush back.

GRANNY: *(Moving to Drinks)* Right. Would you like a drink?

PETER: Please. Whisky would do fine.

GRANNY: *(Pouring whisky)* Are you looking forward to being a poxy God-Father.

PETER: Proxy, Mother, proxy. 'One deputed to act for another'. Poxy: 'Is a disease attended by pustules'. . . . .

GRANNY: You must have been the poxiest teenager I ever saw.

PETER: Really! *(Takes drink and sits down)* Thank you. I'm not really happy about the Christening you know.

GRANNY: *(Pouring herself a whisky)* You'll be all right when you get there. You're suffering from first font nerves.

PETER: I can't understand Jenny.

GRANNY: *(Moving to chair)* I can. Have you ever seen such a beautiful baby?

PETER: I really can't answer that. I believe beauty is in the eye of the beholder.

GRANNY: Try telling that to a mother. For sheer blind devotion, you can't beat mother love. *(Drinks)* You were just about the ugliest thing produced outside Jurassic Park. After your father saw you for the first time, he got tight for a fortnight, and my vibes were on the blink for months. Thank God the midwife advised against breast feeding.

PETER: I though breast feeding was the in thing when I was born.

GRANNY: It was, but that sainted midwife had a theory that you'd get on my tits quite soon enough without me encouraging you.

PETER: Thank you very much mother. Look, aren't you concerned about the Christening? Jenny and Colin aren't married, and they don't seem likely to be in the foreseeable future.

GRANNY: They love each other.

PETER: *(Standing)* They have no legal responsibility to each other. Colin could get up and walk away any day, and that would be that.

GRANNY: Jenny could do the same.

PETER: She wouldn't do that.

GRANNY:I'll tell you one thing Peter, it's a damn sight better to live together in love that to get married for the sake of convention, and then get divorced.

PETER: Yes, yes, that's all very well, but what really gets me is them having the Christening at all in the circumstances.

GRANNY: Has it ever occurred to you, that in their own way, they might believe in God.

PETER: How can they? If they really believed, they'd get married, then they'd have the Christening.

GRANNY: You'd have been a wow in Victorian days. I don't know how you didn't send Rosie round the twist.

ROSIE:*(Above Granny)* Oh he did mum, many times. Especially when the kids were growing up. He hardly ever listened to them, and vary rarely discussed things with them. I know he worked hard, and he'd give them anything... anything except his time. And that's what they needed more than anything.

PETER: Rosie understood me.

GRANNY: *(Getting up and moving towards Peter)* She was about the most understanding person I ever knew. She had to be to have married you. I know it's tough, Peter, but you've got to adjust to the world as it is now... it doesn't have to adjust to you.

PETER: I know but...

GRANNY:... But! But is the worst word in the world and it's not even a four lettered one.

PETER: Deeply philosophical.

GRANNY: *(Patting him gently on the arm)* Tell me, how do you think I felt when you married Rosie?

PETER: Are you trying to tell me you didn't like her? I don't believe what I'm hearing.

GRANNY: Didn't like her? I loved her, Peter.

PETER: Then what are you saying?

GRANNY: I was afraid that you. You who I pushed into this world... and hell, how I pushed... wouldn't be good enough for her.

PETER: And was I?

GRANNY: Only you know that.

ROSIE: I know it, mum. He was, for me he was everything I wanted. Oh, we didn't always see eye to eye. I could be very stubborn, especially in the early days. If I wanted something I nearly always got it, somehow or other. I used to tell him that as a little girl I never had this, or I never had that, because my mother didn't have time for me. That wasn't strictly true, and I'm not very proud of it. Tell him to get on with his life, do his own thing. We've only got one life on earth. I know that... but it's not the end... don't let him waste what he's got left just because I'm not here. I loved him too much for that.

PETER: I feel so inadequate.

GRANNY: Of course you do. We all do at times. Perhaps recognising our inadequacies is one of our strengths. Do you think Rosie would approve of your attitude to Colin?

PETER: As I've said, she'd understand.

GRANNY: Tolerate. It's possible, knowing Rosie that she'd tolerate it, which is, perhaps a form of understanding, but it's a long way from approving. There's only one reason that you don't like Colin, and it's not because he's married to Jenny.

PETER: Yes it is.

GRANNY: Balls!

PETER: Mother, really!

GRANNY: *(Moving to re-fill glasses)* You don't like Colin because at the moment he isn't in the position to fully support Jenny in the way you think she should be supported... you think... not them, they're perfectly happy... but you like sitting on the right hand of God, don't you? And now with the baby you're worried that things will get worse.

PETER: Yes... I am worried. She shouldn't have got mixed up with him. A freelance journalist writing novels is a high risk proposition.

GRANNY:*(Passing him re-filled glass)* Your trouble is you've forgotten about genuine love.

PETER: I was married for over twenty nine years.

GRANNY: That's evading the issue. *(Sits)* I haven't forgotten genuine love. It was wonderful. I can identify with grandchildren. I think we can see the innocence in them... the innocence we used to have. My father didn't understand my marriage, but then he didn't try very hard. He was an unhappy man.

PETER: So am I. *(Peter sits)*

GRANNY: For a very different reason. Bereavement which ever way you look at it, is an awful thing. You lose something, something priceless to you, which you can never fully replace.

PETER: I never knew Grandfather. What was he like?

GRANNY: A late Victorian pain in the ass.

PETER: Strict? Straight laced?

GRANNY: Do you remember Mr Murdstone in David Copperfield.

PETER: Vaguely.

GRANNY: Take a line through him and Herod's attitude to children.

PETER: You're exaggerating.

GRANNY:I always do. It's a simple pleasure, and it doesn't really hurt anybody.

PETER: You don't think I'm like grandfather, do you?

GRANNY: Not yet, but I do detect traits in your character which in your present depressed state need watching.

PETER: Very easy to say, mother.

GRANNY: You ought to get out and join something.

PETER: Like what?

GRANNY: I don't know. How about a Badminton Club?

PETER: I'm not taking up Badminton at my age. I might strain something.

GRANNY: Rambling then.

PETER: Not with my feet.

GRANNY: I know... why don't you join your local dramatic society?

PETER: That is an embarrassing subject, mother.

GRANNY: Oh good, tell me more.

PETER: About a month ago I was at one of Mollie Bellfield's parties, and well... I was feeling a bit down, and I found myself talking to myself. I talk to myself an awful lot since Rosie died. I wonder if other people in my position do? It worries me sometimes... do you know, I had a real argument with a saucepan the other evening.

GRANNY: Did it win?

PETER: It's got an awful dent in it now. I threw it at the wall.

GRANNY: It won. You always were a poor loser, Peter. Come on, what's this about Mollie Bellfield's party?

PETER: Oh yes... well, as I was saying, I was talking to myself. I honestly didn't think anyone would notice. You know what Mollie's parties are like... all chin and chatter. Anyhow, there I was rabbiting on and I looked up and she was staring at me a bit old fashioned.

GRANNY: Like you were out of your tree you mean?

PETER: More or less. Well, to cut a long story short, she asked me what I was doing, and I said the first thing that came into my mind. I told her I was going over my lines for the next dramatic society production.

GRANNY: *(Laughing)* You are a berk, Peter. Oh, I wish I'd been there. Look, why don't you take a woman out? You're not bad looking from a distance.

PETER: How do you take a woman out from a distance? It's no good, mother... I'm just not in the mood. I feel uneasy about... oh you know... relationships. I'm not at all sure that I'm not impotent since Rosie died.

GRANNY: *(Getting up quickly)* Oh my God. Finish your drink and have another one quick. Are you sure about what you said?

PETER: Not really, but I don't seem to have any inclination. *(Peter hands her glass)*

GRANNY: *(Pouring Peter a drink)* It's not catching is it? Have you seen the doctor?

PETER: Good heavens no. It doesn't really worry me. In fact it's one of the least of my worries.

GRANNY: It would terrify me. *(Sits and sips whisky)* Here, you haven't gone gay have you?

PETER: Don't you start. I had quite enough of that from Mollie Bellfield.

GRANNY: Sounds interesting. What did she say?

PETER: In no uncertain terms she hinted that it happens to a lot of men in my position.

GRANNY: Does she know a lot of men in your position?

PETER: I've no idea, but you know what an airhead Mollie is.

GRANNY: True. Once her figure went there wasn't much else to go. Was Val Malkin there?

PETER: Definitely.

GRANNY: She always fancied you you know.

ROSIE: Peter fancied her once. Mind you, he'd had more than a few. I think it was our first real row. I was going through post natal depression and he was doubting the wisdom of one of the commandments.

PETER: Mother, Val Markin fancies anything in trousers, male or female.

GRANNY: Fair comment, but don't forget the poor soul is married to James.

PETER: Please don't start matchmaking. I am really not interested, and even if I was, I wouldn't be interested in Val Markin. It would be like going out with an octopus.

GRANNY: You miss Rosie terribly, don't you?

PETER:*(Deep sigh)* You know, we could sit for ages and not say a word, and it would be better than any conversation. Do I miss her? What do you think?

GRANNY: It's quite unimportant what I think. What is important is the way you think. Readjustment is terribly difficult.

PETER: How long does it take?

GRANNY: In time as we know it? I think that's un-answerable.

PETER: I suppose you're right. It's something I've got to do myself, for myself, isn't it?

GRANNY: Yes. *(Pause)* I've been there you know.

PETER: Good God! So you have. I never think of you as a widow.

GRANNY: And the sooner you stop thinking of yourself as a widower, the better. The world doesn't owe you a lifetime of sympathy.

ROSIE: Good for you mum. Something might get through eventually. It's got to... for his sake.

PETER: *(Getting up)* Mum...

GRANNY: *(Looking at Peter as he stands there)* Mum... that's the first time you've called me mum for a very long time. Mum... it makes me feel sort of warm, comfortable, useful even. Instinctively mum's love their sons, and some of the sons love their mums, at least for a time... then they experience the teenage menopause, and sadly, sometimes forever, the umbilical cord is broken.

PETER: Have I been like that?

GRANNY: Perhaps... should I judge? Anyhow, something that's been broken can often be mended.

PETER: Can it?

GRANNY: If the people want it.

PETER: Mum...

GRANNY:/(Getting up and crossing to Peter)* You poor old darling... you hurt, don't you?

PETER: Yes.

GRANNY: *(Embracing him)* It gets easier, believe me... but you have to contribute the majority of the effort.

(They hold the embrace. Lights fade on Peter and Granny. Lights up on Colin who enters carrying two glasses of wine.)

COLIN: Granny, here's another glass of that wine you liked last time you were here. We got it in specially.

(Granny who has taken off cardigan during light fade now walks into Colin's scene)

GRANNY: Oh thank you dear. *(Takes glass)* tell me, Colin... what's a sureity?

COLIN: I'm not all that sure myself. Some horse that never wins a race I think.

GRANNY: Really? *(Takes a drink as Peter walks into scene)* Peter, do you know that you've just promised your God-son that he'll never win a race?

PETER: What on earth are you talking about, mother?

COLIN: Not only that, Peter, but you've promised that he will renounce the devil and all his works.

PETER: Did I? I can't recall saying a single word. I thought I'd have to make some sort of declaration.

GRANNY: God parents don't have to say anything, they just stand there and look affluent.

JENNY: *(Entering with glass of wine)* Daddy made a good attempt at looking affluent, didn't you, darling. Of course Slade Dorval is affluent, but he doesn't look it.

PETER: What does this Slade Dorval look like?

COLIN: Did you ever see Lon Chaney as 'The Wolf Man?'

PETER: No.

COLIN: Well you wouldn't recognise him then.

JENNY: Don't be rotten, Colin. Slade is... well from your point of view Daddy, he'd be untidy, scruffy, undisciplined, but strangely attractive. Do you know what I mean?

GRANNY: A bit of rough.

COLIN: As a matter of fact he's a B.A.

PETER: He sounds it.

JENNY: Bachelor of Arts, Daddy.

PETER: I'm impressed. What in?

COLIN: English literature. He's writing a thesis on the development of folk music from Greensleeves to the Sex Pistols.

GRANNY: I used to like that.

PETER: What, The Sex Pistols?

GRANNY: Don't be silly, Peter. Greensleeves. I always imagined Henry the Eighth playing on his lute then nipping off to the Royal Bedchamber for a quickie.

JENNY: Come on Granny, let's go and see if the baby is all right. *(They exit Right)*

PETER: Colin, can I have a word with you?

COLIN: Of course you can.

PETER: I wanted to thank you for changing the baby's last name to Peter.

COLIN: You like Zechariah Ezra Peter?

PETER: Not a hundred per cent... but Jenny told me that you changed the last name from Paul to Peter, and that it was entirely your idea and nothing whatsoever to do with her.

COLIN: It was to do with her, in as much as you are her father, and she loves you. It seemed a simple enough gesture to me.

PETER: Thank you, Colin. It would have meant a great deal to Rosie.

COLIN:I know I'm not your ideal son-in-law, in fact of course, I'm not your son-in-law at all... not yet... but couldn't we... shouldn't we make the effort?

PETER: I'm going to need a lot of help Colin. Can you provide some of it?

COLIN: It won't be for the want of trying. Thank you, Peter.

PETER: Thank you, Colin. *(They chink glasses. The lights slowly fade on Peter and Colin)*

Curtain

ACT II

A month later. Bring up lights on pub down stage right. Louisa, the landlady is picking up empty glasses from the table.

VOICE: *(Offstage)*, Louisa, pint of bitter.

(Peter enters stage left, crosses and sits at table)

LOUISA: Hello, Peter, you're early. *(moves to exit)* Shan't be a minute, old Norman's having withdrawal symptoms. He finished his first pint over twenty seconds ago.

PETER: I'll have a whisky whilst you're in there.

LOUISA: Right. *(exits)*

PETER: Thanks. *(Takes diary from pocket and thumbs through it)* What on earth did I promise to get for Colin's birthday? I thought I'd written it down. I ought to write everything down these days. I can't remember a damn thing, and I used to have such a good memory before Rosie died. Oh, blast it, what was it? *(Looks in diary)* It's his birthday next Friday. Why did I promise to go there for the week-end? I'd be better off on my own... I don't feel like company... especially Colin's. He's hard work, there's no two ways about it. *(Puts diary back in pocket)* I ought to make more of an effort for Jenny's sake, I know I should. Still. It was nice of her to ask me I suppose... but I wish she hadn't. *(Louisa stands upstage watching Peter. She has his whisky with her).* She's a good kid though. She misses her mother, I know she does. Oh, Rosie, why did you have to die?

LOUISA:*(Moving to table)* Here's your whisky, Peter. Thank the power's that be Sandra's arrived. She's serving Norman. *(She sits at table)* What's up?

PETER: *(paying Louisa)* Nothing. Why?

LOUISA: Chattering away to yourself like a wagon load of monkeys. Mind you, you don't fall out with anyone that way.

PETER: You do you know. Quite often. There are times when I don't feel like myself at all. I often have a really good go at myself, especially if I'm looking in a mirror.

LOUISA: I think all of us do that sort of thing at times.

PETER: Not like I do. I really mean it. I know what I've become Louisa, and I don't care for it at all. I know what I want to be but there doesn't seem to be any point to it. *(Drinks)* and does it matter anyway?

LOUISA: Come on, Peter, this isn't like you.

PETER: It's more like me than the other side I present. That's an act... I've become a bloody act... a hollow shell... a facade. Life goes on, everyone tells you that, but they don't tell you how to cope with it. Do you know, just after Rosie died, I used to go round telling myself that people were admiring me... 'Look at old Peter, he's taken it marvellously. Hasn't lost his sense of humour... just gets on with life' It used to give me a lift, in fact it got so I really believed my own lies... until I got home... then I knew the truth... and the hurting began, and it's still there, still there.

LOUISA: To thine own self be true. I don't know who said it, but there's a lot of truth in it.

PETER: *(Taking a drink)* Sorry, I shouldn't have gone on like that. I've had a bad day, and on top of that I've forgotten what I promised to get my son-in-law for his birthday.

LOUISA: Well, that's easy enough. Just ring Jenny and ask her what it was.

PETER: I can't do that, she'd think I didn't care. She's very touchy about my relationship with Colin. They're not married you know.

LOUISA: So what?

PETER: I don't approve of it.

LOUISA: You know, for a man who gives generously to charity, you're not very charitable. If they love each other, what's it got to do with you whether they are married or not?

PETER: My mother said more or less the same thing. Nobody seems to care about my opinion.

LOUISA: Nobody will care about you, period, if you take that attitude.

PETER: There's nothing wrong with my attitude. Don't you understand what it's like to...

LOUISA: *(Standing up)* Don't bother to explain Peter, I'll borrow my husband's word processor and write a novel about it. *(Moving towards exit)*

PETER: That's it. Word processor! God bless you Louisa. *(Takes a drink)*

LOUISA: What are you talking about?

PETER: Word processor. That's what I promised Jenny I'd get Colin for his birthday.

LOUISA: Bit over the top isn't it.

PETER: Well he is my...

LOUISA: No he's not, they're not married. Why are you giving him a word processor?

PETER: I've told you, it's his birthday.

LOUISA: Tell me, are you giving it because you want to, or are you giving it because you know it will impress Jenny? Are you really giving it to Colin?

PETER: Of course I am.

LOUISA: Would you give it to him if it wasn't for Jenny?

PETER: If it wasn't for Jenny, I wouldn't know him.

LOUISA: Fair point. It's an expensive present though, especially for someone you don't approve of.

PETER: There's a special offer down at Royston's.

LOUISA: Even so it's a good bit more than the usual birthday present, especially close to Christmas.

PETER: Louisa, I am giving the word processor to Colin because I want him to like me. Can you understand that? I want to be liked... is that such a bad thing?

LOUISA: It's a gesture to Rosie. That's how I see it. You know she wouldn't approve of your attitude to Colin, so you're...

PETER: Is that fair, Louisa?

LOUISA: You tell me.

PETER:I don't know. I don't think I know anything anymore. Jenny said it would be a great help to Colin...

LOUISA: So you thought... here's a great chance to impress. Make a grand gesture... obligate him...

PETER: I'm pathetic aren't I? Transparent even. Do you know he changed the baby's third name from Paul to Peter after me... that was a wonderful thing to do... and I've tried, I've really tried to like him... but all I seem to be capable of is to make material gesture in return... Is that all I'm capable of giving? Have I lost the ability, and the capacity to love?

LOUISA:I somehow doubt it, but I must say you're doing a hell of a good job at hiding it.

VOICE: *(Offstage)* Louisa, the Bass has gone, can you come and change the barrel?

LOUISA: All right Sandra, coming. *(Moves to exit)* Sit there quiet for while, Peter... it might do some good. *(Exits)*

(Peter finishes his drink. Gets up and exits left. Fade lights on Pub scene. Lights up on rostrum. Peter enters and as he does so the door bell rings. He looks annoyed exits left to answer.)

PETER: *(Offstage)* Oh good Lord... it's you Fiona. *(Re-enters)* What do you want?

FIONA: *(A good looking woman mid to late forties. Very pseudo dramatic in manner)*

Your body, darling.

PETER: Don't be pathetic. I'm not on your wave length.

FIONA: *(Taking off her coat and sitting in Peter's chair.)* And your mind.

PETER: Are you off your trolley. *(Takes her coat)* Do you want a drink?

FIONA: Lovely. I'll have a scotch.

PETER: *(Moves towards left exit. Sarcastically says)* Do sit down.

FIONA: I'm not interrupting anything, am I?

PETER: *(Offstage)* What is there to interrupt?

FIONA: Good question. I suppose everything is so different now?

PETER: *(Re-entering. Moves to drinks and pours whisky for Fiona and* *himself.)* Of course it is. Everything changes you know. For years we don't think it will... then it happens.*(hands drink to Fiona)*

FIONA: Thank you, Peterkins.

PETER: *(Drawing up, upright chair and sitting)* Don't call me Peterkins. To what do I owe this dubious pleasure of this visit? Not many people come to see me now.

FIONA: I had coffee with Mollie Bellfield this morning.

PETER: How the other half lives.

FIONA: We all know she's many p short of a pound darling, but what's this she was telling me about you taking part in the next dramatic production.

PETER: I'd rather not talk about it.

FIONA: *(Drinks)* But your going to.

PETER: No I'm not.

FIONA: Why were you talking to yourself, Peterkins? Mollie said you reminded her of an over stimulated goldfish.

PETER: Oh, I don't know. Yes, I do... I tend to talk to myself quite a lot now.

FIONA: I talk to myself every morning at breakfast.

PETER: Doesn't Brian eat breakfast?

FIONA: Yes, but he doesn't speak. He grunts on occasions, but you can't have a proper conversation with a grunt. Why did you tell Mollie that you'd joined the dramatic society?

PETER: It was the first thing that came into my mind. I can tell you, it was damned embarrassing.

FIONA: Brilliant.

PETER: I beg your pardon?

FIONA: Darling, don't you see, it means that your sub-conscious is yearning to be an actor.

PETER: Absolute rubbish.

FIONA: It is not. It's a shining example of root motivation.

PETER: Fiona, what in the hell are you talking about?

FIONA: I need you.

PETER: Why, do you want to sell your house?

FIONA: Of course I don't.

PETER: It was a logical question. I am an Estate Agent.

FIONA: Estate Agents aren't logical. I happen to be producing the next play, and you are only fabulously ideal for one of the supporting roles.

PETER: No way. I've only ever been on the stage once in my life, and that was an Infant School Nativity, and the Inn Keeper wet himself.

FIONA: You won't wet yourself.

PETER: You bet I won't, because I'm not getting involved.

FIONA: You are. You need the challenge, the outside interest. Rosie would agree if she was here.

ROSIE: *(behind Peter's chair)* Fiona's perfectly right. He needs something to occupy his mind. He's getting far too moody and insular.

FIONA: You're getting moody and insular.

ROSIE: She must have been listening.

PETER: No I'm not. And even if I was, how would you know, you haven't seen me for yonks.

FIONA: Of course I haven'. Why should I?

PETER: Well I...

FIONA: Mollie Bellfield and Val Malkin mentioned it.

PETER: It's got nothing to do with them.

FIONA: They're worried about you.

PETER: They've got a funny way of showing it. In any case they don't need to be.

ROSIE: Such a gracious attitude. If he goes round like that nobody will bother about him and I don't blame them.

FIONA: Peter, that's not very nice.

ROSIE: It certainly isn't. If he'd behaved like that when I was alive, he'd have known all about it. He makes me so angry at times. I know what he'll do now, he'll hide behind his grief.

PETER: Sorry. *(Deep sigh)* It's just that things have a different perspective these days. There are times, too many times, especially when I'm alone, when nothing seems to make any real sense.

FIONA: There you are then. Acting is just the thing for you. The less sense a play makes, the better the critics like it.

PETER: There are times Fiona, and I fully admit it, when Rosie used to confuse me... but you are in a class of your own.

FIONA: You were saying that there are times now when nothing makes real sense. Well, there you are then... acting isn't real.

PETER: What is it then?

FIONA: It's acting... performing on a stage or screen. One who plays a part in an outstanding event.

PETER: You sound like a dictionary.

FIONA: That's where I got it from. Anyhow, you get the essence of what I'm saying, don't you, Peterkins?

PETER: No.

FIONA: One who plays a part. Whichever way you look at it, that's pretending. It isn't real. And if you ask me, in your present state, that's what you need. You need to become somebody else.

PETER: I wish I was somebody else at this moment.

FIONA: *(Getting up)*That's the spirit. First rehearsal Thursday evening at the Barminster Social Club, seven thirty.

PETER: I shan't be there.

FIONA: I wouldn't bet on it. Where's my jacket?

PETER: I'll get it. *(Starts to exit left)*.

FIONA: Thank you Peterkins. *(Moving after him)* Lots to do. I must be running along.

PETER: Good.

FIONA: Oh, by the way, my Uncle Roger is coming down tomorrow for a few days. Au revoir Peterkins, Darling. *(Kisses him on cheek. This is said on the way offstage)*

ROSIE: Nice one, Fiona.

PETER: That woman get's crazier by the minute.

EVANGELIST:*(Entering stage right to just right of rostrum)* Good evening my friend. May I enquire if you have found Jesus?

PETER: *(Moving quickly towards him)* You were here about a month ago, has he been missing all that time?

EVANGELIST: I beg your pardon?

PETER: You were looking for him a month ago. He's not here. I don't take house guests.

EVANGELIST: I've been here before have I?

PETER: Yes. You called in the morning that time. What's this Evensong?

EVANGELIST: Ah! Now I remember. You're the atheist.

PETER: I'm not an atheist.

EVANGELIST: Pity.

PETER: What?

EVANGELIST: You get a deeper discussion with an atheist. They always seem to have stronger arguments than I do. You see, I'm pretty new to this sort of thing. During my first week an atheist practically convinced me that I didn't exist. Fascinating! I've had doubts ever since.

PETER: How wonderfully boring. I have things to do.

EVANGELIST: Certainly. *(Moves stage left)* Well, good evening to you. I will call again in about a month. Perhaps you'll be able to convince me that I do exist. God be with you. Goodbye. *(Exits left)*.

PETER:*(Moving back to Rostrum)* Fiona Frobisher and a demented bible basher who doubts his own existence. *(Pours himself a whisky)* I wonder what Fiona really wanted? She can't be serious about a play. Hah! If she thinks she can twist me round her little finger she's got another think coming.

ROSIE: Fiona's far too smart for you, Peter. It may take her some time, but she always gets her own way.

PETER:*(Sitting in armchair)* I'm fed up. *(Feels his pulse)* Oh! Bit jumpy. *(Feels pulse again)* Yes... definitely. *(Feels his heart)* Oh! Goodness, it's got a rumba beat. *(Takes a drink)*Phew! I'm sweating. *(Dabs forehead with handkerchief)* I think I've got a fever. *(Loosens his tie)* I'll go and see Doc Reynolds in the morning... oh no, can't just drop in. I'll have to make an appointment. Yes, that's what I'll do. Haven't had a check up since Rosie died. Phew! Dear oh dear... dizzy spell... steady on... sit perfectly still. *(Two or three deep breaths)* Aaah! That's better.

ROSIE: I do believe he's getting back to normal. He hasn't had a touch of hypochondria for months. I've been quite worried about him. Too busy with his sorrow symptons I suppose. Of course that's better than when he was really ill. Bit on the inconvenient side at times, especially that week-end when he took to his bed the first time my mother came to stay. I was never really sure about that little episode.

PETER: I'll have an early night. *(Looks at his watch and gets up)* I'll take an aspirin, they say it's good for the heart. *(Tops up whisky and moves to exit left)* And whisky helps thin the blood, I think. *(Kisses Rosies photograph)* Right, I'm off to bed. *(Exits left)*.

(Lights down on rostrum. Lights up on Dr Reynolds Surgery. Reynolds is seated at desk writing. This scene is where Granny's room was situated in act one. Peter enters stage left above office and moves down to desk.)

REYNOLDS: Hello Peter. Haven't seen you for some time. Not been well?

PETER: *(Sitting in patients chair)* I'm not too bad.

REYNOLDS: Then what are you doing here?

PETER: I'm depressed.

REYNOLDS: You're depressed! You want to try sitting here day after day. Do you know, I haven't got a healthy patient on my registers. This particular surgery started at half past five, and it is now a quarter past six. I have already had two hypochondriacs... tell me what do you prescribe for the patient that's got everything? Then there was an in growing toe nail job... that was easy, refered him straight to the hospital... and then just before you came in here, there was a young woman complaining that she hadn't seen anythin for three months, and I was so bemused from the hypochondriacs, that I was writing a note out for the opticians before I realised that what she really needed was a pregnancy test. Anyhow, enough of my tribulations, how are you?

PETER: I was hoping you were going to tell me that.

REYNOLDS: What a quaint idea.

PETER: Oh come on Bill, you're the doctor.

REYNOLDS: All right, all right, what are the symptons?

PETER: I don't seem to have any real energy. I'm tired, but it's not a pleasant tiredness. Things I could always cope with tend to get on top of me. And I've lost over a stone and a half.

REYNOLDS: Yes you have, haven't you? Ah well, at least I shan't have to put you on a diet. That's becoming almost obligatory you know.

PETER: The weight went very suddenly.

REYNOLDS: The shock of losing Rosie.

PETER: Then why did it take so long? She's been gone over a year. I honestly thought I'd got the big C.

REYNOLDS: Why didn't you come and see me then?

PETER: I was scared.

REYNOLDS: Pretty normal reaction to thinking you've got cancer. Anyhow, loss of weight is very normal thing in bereavement cases. *(Gets up and moves round to front of desk. Sits on Desk)* It's the shock coming out, and you can never tell with shock. In the course of time it will leave the body, but there's no way of knowing how long the process will take. Two years is agood average, but that's all it is, an average. Everyone reacts differently. Anyhow you don't want to worry about that, you were getting to be a proper porker the last time I saw you. Sleeping well?

PETER: Pretty reasonable.

REYNOLDS: Do you take sleeping tablets?

PETER: No, but I always have a whisky before I go to bed.

REYNOLDS: Better than anything I can give you. Eating all right?

PETER: No problems. Even though I cook most of it myself, I normally enjoy my food.

REYNOLDS: Bowels regular?

PETER: Very.

REYNOLDS: You're in better shape than I am.

PETER: I don't feel it.

REYNOLDS: How do you know how I feel?

PETER: Well obviously I don't, but you know what I mean. I get worried about my mind sometimes.

REYNOLDS: What's the matter with it?

PETER: If I'm on my own for any length of time, I become sort of emeshed in memories. You see, everytime I go home from work, or from seeing friends, or anything like that, I go into an empty house, and the memories I'm getting lately, well, the bad ones are getting to predominate.

REYNOLDS: Good. Get 'em out in the open... don't bottle them up. A trouble shared is a trouble halved. It's an old saying, and there isn't all that much truth in it, but it does help.

PETER:I've been noticing peoples reactions and there's another old saying with a lot of truth in it. 'A friend in need is a bloody nuisance!'.

REYNOLDS: There was always a cynical side to you, Peter.

PETER: *(Getting up)* I suppose the real truth is that I feel guilty about Rosie dying. I keep thinking... 'If only I'd done this, if only I'd done that...

REYNOLDS: *(Moving towards Peter)* There is absolutely no point in thinking along those lines.

PETER:I keep telling myself that. But it doesn't seem to help. Some days all the memories I have of Rosie are terrific, but at other times, this guilt thing comes roaring back, and I mean roaring. I think that's the reason, the real reason why I'm here talking to you.

REYNOLDS: If you think talking to me will help,then it probably will, but let me give you a word of advice, as a friend, not as a doctor. Unless you consciously make an effort to stop blaming yourself for something, which deep down at least, you must know you had absolutely no control over, then you're in the catch 22 position. Bereavement is a very personal thing, and the only person who can lastingly help you is yourself. It's a long, lonely battle, and nobody else can win it except yourself.

PETER: That's more or less what I've been telling myself.

REYNOLDS:*(Moving back and sitting in chair)* Then you're ahead of the game. All you've got to do is get on with it.

PETER: That's the problem Bill, I don't know how to.*(Sits)* Tell me how to do it.

REYNOLDS: If only I could.

PETER: Can't you give me something?

REYNOLDS: Nobody has ever invented a tablet for your complaint. Tell me, what do you do when you've finished work for the day?

PETER: Call in the pub for a couple of drinks, bit of company. Go home, cook a meal, watch television, then go to bed.

REYNOLDS: Don't you belong to any organisations or clubs?

PETER: Only the cricket club, but that's shut all the winter.

REYNOLDS: Peter, since you became a widower, you have to all intents and purposes become like someone who moves house to a completely new location. You don't know where you are. You don't know what you want. You have to go out and find the answers... you can't sit around and expect them to come to you. For your own sake, go out and join something. Get yourself involved in something you haven't been involved in before. Make the effort Peter, or it'll get tougher and tougher.

PETER: Can it? I thought the old adage was 'it'll get easier'.

REYNOLDS: I believe we should attempt to learn something every day, otherwise there's no point to the day. Those two hypochondriacs have taught me something which might help you.

PETER: Grasping at straws aren't you?

REYNOLDS:I don't think so. Those two people left this surgery contented, and
they were contented because I gave them prescriptions for something which
won't cure the ailment they haven't got, but they believe it will.

PETER: You want me to become a hypochondriac?

REYNOLDS:I want you to adapt, Peter. Instead of using the old 'Oh, there's a lot
of people worse off than I am',syndrome... Say to yourself 'I'm a lot worse off
than a lot of other people'... and be thankful. There's nothing wrong with a
dollop of self pity, provided you don't over do it.

PETER:*(Getting up)*Okay Bill. *(Moves to exit)* I'll give it some thought, but I'm
not over optimistic.

REYNOLDS: Then you won't be disappointed if it doesn't work, will you? Come
and see me in another month.

PETER: All right. Night Bill. *(Exits)*

REYNOLDS:I sometimes wonder if the hippocratic oath is all it's cracked up to
be.

*(Fade lights on Reynolds. Lights up on rostrum. Rosie is standing slightly
downstage right of rostrum in spot light.)*

ROSIE: Has he taken one step forward and two back? Difficult to tell with
someone like Peter. There was always a side to him which he never completely
revealed in all the years I knew him. Still, the doctor was right... he needs to
be more positive. He was positive when I was alive. Too positive at one stage,
when the kids were growing up. Business, business, business. Financially it
was good, but it put a strain on our marriage for a time. I seriously considered
divorcing him... he never had time for any of us... but I'm glad I didn't... Still
he's got to do something now. The more he does the less time he'll have to
think about the past. He was always a great one for nostalgia. He never
realised the best thing about nostalgia is that it's gone.*(Moves onto Rostrum
above armchair)*.

PETER:*(Enters stage left. Pours himself s drink. Sits in armchair).* You'd have
thought Bill would have given me a tonic or something. It's not like the old
days.

ROSIE: Good job for him it isn't. They'd have covered him in leeches or amputated something.

PETER: *(Looks at watch)* Only seven o'clock. What a drag of a day. I ought to get something to eat I suppose. *(Gets up)* Oh hell! I don't feel hungry, I can't be bothered. *(Tops up his glass)* This won't do any good, but at least it's no hassle to prepare.

ROSIE: Bill Reynolds should never have said that bit about self pity. He's in one of those moods where the whole world's against him. Oh, I've lived through a few of them. He used to get right up my nose. Ah well, best let the old fool get on with it. *(Exits)*

PETER: What's on the box? *(Picks up magazine. Looks at it)* Oh! That's typical isn't it? Three repeats of shows that weren't worth watching in the first place and a documentary on The Dung Beetle and it's Natural Habitat. *(Throws the magazine on floor. Door bell rings)* Who the hell is that? *(Moves stage Left)*Oh, good Lord, what do you want?

FIONA: *(Offstage)* Peterkins, darling, what a lovely welcome.

(Peter andf Fiona enter. Fiona crosses to magazine picks it up and puts it on the table. Smiles at Peter)

FIONA: Can't abide magazines on the floor, darling. I'm glad you're in.

PETER: Where did you expect me to be? There's no place to go... not for me.

FIONA: There's going to be though, isn't there?

PETER: No.

FIONA: Wrong Peterkins, wrong. I've just been talking to Uncle Roger.

PETER: About as interesting as tonight's television.

FIONA: You're edgy tonight, Peter. I told you he was coming down for a few days, well, he wants to see you.

PETER: What does he want to see me about? I've never met the man.

FIONA: You know Carrington Terrace

PETER: Of course I know it. Very prestidious.

FIONA: He owns it.

PETER: Oh! Oh, does he?

FIONA: He wants advice on selling it. I recommended you.

PETER: I should have thought he would have gone to one of the big agencies.

FIONA: He would have done, darling, only I happen to be his favourite niece, and for some reason he has always confided in me, and he always asks my advice. He thinks I've got a calculating mind.

PETER: Uncle Roger is no fool.

FIONA: He wants to see you the day after tomorrow *(Smiles)* It'll give you a chance to get over your first rehearsal.

PETER: Fiona, I have no intentions of appearing in your stupid play.

FIONA: You're just playing hard to get. If you don't come to rehearsals...

PETER: Well?

FIONA: Don't bother to come and see Uncle Roger, He'll be right off you by the time I've finished your character assassination.

PETER: But that's blackmail.

FIONA: Absolutely darling. *(Pats his cheek)* It's fun isn't it *(Moves to exit)* Uncle Roger is very keen on the theatre, so you'll have lots in common, won't you? It's always a good thing to have something in common with a client, apart from business. Chaio! *(Exits)*.

PETER: The bitch!

(Cut lights on rostrum. Lights up on Susan and Gerald. They have just come in from an evening out and are taking off coats.)

SUSAN: I know it's terrific from a prospects point of view Gerald, but...

GERALD:... There aren't any 'buts' Sue. Janner says we fly to New York on the 23rd to represent the dear old company, so we fly.

SUSAN: It's the twentieth today. What are we going to do about Peter?

GERALD: Oh good heavens, do you know the excitement of it all completely drove father out of my head.

SUSAN: He'll be on his own for Christmas, what are we going to do?

GERALD: There's nothing we can do. He'll understand. After all he's in business himself. He knows one can't afford to let any opportunity slip these days for any reason, including Christmas and widowed fathers.

(Cut lights on Susan and Gerald. Lights up on rostrum. Peter is seated in armchair holding a list in his hands)

PETER:... right, that's Jenny, Colin and the baby seen to... Mother... *(Looks at list)* What on earth can I get for my Mother? Oh dear, oh dear, let's face it, Christmas isn't all beer and skittles. I'll have to think of something... but what? Gerald, that's all right, I've got his... Susan? Oh dammit, she's more difficult than Mother. I've got to get her something, I can't arrive there empty handed.

(Studies list. Cut lights on rostrum. Lights up on Susan and Gerald)

SUSAN: *(Picking up telephone)* I'll give Granny a ring.

GERALD: What for?

SUSAN: To see if she can have Peter. I can't bear to think of him on his own, not at Christmas.

GERALD: Well we're not doing it on purpose. Come on Sue, he's not a child you know.

SUSAN: Isn't he?

GERALD: Do you know where my passport is?

SUSAN: The last time I saw it it was in the drawer of the bedside table.

GERALD: I'll go and have a look.

(He exits. Spotlight on space where Mandy's flower shop was in act one. Telephone rings once or twice then Granny enters with mobile phone stands in spotlight)

GRANNY: Hello, Christine Mason speaking.

SUSAN: Granny... it's Susan.

GRANNY: Oh, hello dear, lovely to hear from you.

SUSAN: *(Taking a deep breath and speaking rather quickly)* Granny, can you have Peter for Christmas?

GRANNY: It *was* lovely to hear from you. I thought he was going to you.

SUSAN: He was, but Gerald and I have to go New York... very unexpected business trip. All last minute rush, but you know what these big companies are like... perople don't matter.

GRANNY: Have you phoned Jenny?

SUSAN: No, not yet, I didn't want to, what with the new baby and everything. Oh Granny, it really upsets me to think of Peter on his own.

(Fade lights on Susan and Granny. Lights up on rostrum)

PETER: OK, that's it then. *(Checks list)* Let's have a little think for a minute. Right... I can put all the presents in the holdall, then I'll only need one suitcase. *(Gets up. Picks up Rosie's photograph)* I'll take you with me Rosie. *(Kisses photograph)*

ROSIE: I do wish he'd wipe the photograph after he does that.

(Cut lights on rostrum. Lights up on Susan and Granny)

GRANNY: Susan, normally speaking I'd have him here... not that he's exactly the gift wrapped spirit of Christmas, but I shan't be home. I'm going skiing.

SUSAN: Skiing!?

GRANNY: That's right dear, I've always wanted to go.

SUSAN: It's a bit of a sudden decision isn't it?

GRANNY: Yes, well you see the areobics class I belong to had a last minute cancellation because Mrs Hanley ruptured herself doing the splits.

SUSAN: *(Wincing)* Oh dear, how painful.

GRANNY: You'll have to ask Jenny and Colin dear. I mean, he is her father, and if they fill him up with Scotch, he'll be quite tolerable.

SUSAN: All right Granny, I'll give Jenny a ring. I must go there's so much to do. And have a nice time, skiing can be dangerous.

GRANNY: From what I've been told it's the ski instructors you have to be careful of. I do hope the rumours are right. Have a good time in New York, and a happy Christmas.

SUSAN: And to you, Granny.

(They put down their telephones. Cut lights on Granny)

SUSAN: Granny skiing... whatever next. *(Looks at telephone, picks it up again)* The sooner I get it over the better, but I wish my stomach wasn't so knotted.

(Pushes buttons on telephone. Lights up on rostrum,. Telephone rings. Peter answers it)

PETER: Hello, Peter Mason.

SUSAN: Peter, it's Susan here. How are you?

PETER: Fine. Looking forward to seeing you and Gerald. Only a couple of days now. I've practically finished my Christmas shopping. Oh, I'm ever so glad you've rung, I was just thinking about you.

SUSAN: Something nice I hope.

PETER: Can you tell me what you want for Christmas?

SUSAN: Well actually... that's what I've rung about.

PETER: Oh good, because I haven't got a clue what to get you.

SUSAN: Peter... Gerald and I are being sent to New York on the 23rd. We shall be there for four or five days... Peter...

PETER:... You mean...?

SUSAN: We shan't be here for Christmas.

PETER: Oh... I see... that means that I'll be... It's good for Gerald though, isn't it?

SUSAN: Practically certain to mean promotion. He can't refuse it, Peter.

PETER: No... no of course not. You've got to look after number one these days.

SUSAN: You... you'll be all right, won't you?

PETER: Oh yes. I mean, I manage every other day. Christmas is only another day.

SUSAN: Perhaps you could go to Jenny's?

PETER: Don't know. Possible I suppose. I'll be all right, don't worry about me. Eh... well then... have a safe journey.

SUSAN: Thank you, Peter. I'll give you a call as soon as we get back. Perhaps we can spend New Year together.

PETER: Yes... well... we'll have to see... thank you for ringing. Happy Christmas.

SUSAN: And you, Peter. Bye bye. *(Puts telephone down and shakes her head)* Happy Christmas? *(Cut lights as she exits left).*

PETER: Bye. *(Stares at receiver. Replaces it. Slumps into armchair).*

ROSIE: You miserable old sod, Peter. That was a tough call for Susan to make. You notice your son didn't make it. He takes after you in a lot of ways.

PETER: What the hell am I going to do? I was banking on going there this Christms. Everything was arranged. It's too damn bad, it really is.

ROSIE: You've got plenty of friends, why don't you go and inflict yourself on them. On the other hand, with a bit of effort you could look after yourself, it wouldn't kill you. You're behaving just like a spoiled child. There are times when I go right off you.

PETER:I suppose I'll have to look after myself. Too late to book a hotel that's for certain. Oh god... I've never been on my own for Christmas... not in the whole of my life. What do I do? Just sit round? Do I have to cook a bloody great turkey just for myself. And all those sodding sprouts. I can't face it.

ROSIE: He's a bundle of fun when things don't go exactly the way he thinks they ought to. I must have spoiled him.

PETER: Rosie spoiled me that's the trouble.

ROSIE: I knew it wouldn't be his fault.

PETER: I wonder if Jenny knows I'm on my own?

ROSIE: If she doesn't she'll soon find out. He never had much of a stiff upper lip.

PETER:*(Moving to telephone)* I'll give her a ring. *(Pause)* No, I can't do that, it'll look as if I'm inviting myself.

ROSIE: That's exactly how I'd describe it.

PETER: I'll phone her tomorrow.

ROSIE: And trust the jungle drums will have got the message through to her, then she'll ring him, then he can do his big 'Oh, I couldn't possibly put you to all that trouble' act.

PETER:*(Suddenly shouting)* It's not fair. Nobody gives a goddamn! And that's the truth. To hell with them... see if I care.

(Cut lights on rostrum. Lights up on Colin seated at his word processor. He is on the telephone)

COLIN:... rightho Susan... yes of course I'll tell Jen. Have a safe trip. All the best to Gerald. Happy Christmas. Bye now.*(Puts the telephone down. Picks up* *memo pad)* Now then, let's get this clear. My mum is comimg on the 23rd... she's half a household on her own. It's Zech's first Christmas, still he won't know much about that... and now Peter.

I hope it won't be too much for Jen. We'll have to hope that Peter isn't too edgy and difficult. Booze! *(Makes note on pad)* I'll have to get more in than I was going to. Right, now what was I going to do? Oh yes, 'phone Peter. *(Baby gives a loud cry offstsage)* Oh blast it! *(Moves to exit right)* Oh God! Don't let it be a nappy change. *(Exits. Cut lights on Colin).*

(Lights up on Pub. Peter is seated at table. Louisa enters with a whisky)

LOUISA: Here's your whisky, Peter.Not long now. It's a lot of fuss for a few days isn't it?

PETER: It isn't what it used to be that's for sure.

LOUISA: Still it'll be nice to see Gerald and Susasn, won't it?

PETER: They're going to New York, unexpected business trip. I shall be on my own.

VOICE: *(Offstage)* Louisa!

LOUISA:*(Moving to exit)* Oh, what a shame for you. Coming Charlie! *(Exits).*

(Fiona enters stage left as Peter takes a drink.)

FIONA: Darling, how lovely to see you.

PETER: Fiona, what on earth are you doing here?

FIONA: *(Sitting at table with Peter)* Hoping some kind gentleman will buy me a drink.

PETER: Where's Brian?

FIONA: Gone to the 'Funny-Hand' gang. He said he'd pick me up when he'd rolled his trouser's down. We're going to a party.

PETER: *(moving to exit)* What'll you have?

FIONA: Campari and soda, please.

PETER: Campari and soda please Louisa, when you've got a moment. *(Moves back to table and sits)*

FIONA: Peterkins, I'm having trouble with my parts.

PETER: What are you talking about?

FIONA: Reggie Thorven as called off, and Samantha Bishop is practically certain that she is going to have to have an abortion.

PETER: What's this got to do with me?

FIONA:I wanted you to know that I'm cancelling rehearsals until two weeks after Christmas, so you'll have all that much longer to learn your lines.

PETER: Fiona, I'm not at all happy...

FIONA: Of course you're not, darling. It must be a very trying time of year for you. I mean, obviously it can't be easy, but there's nothing one can do about it, is there?

PETER: No.

FIONA:I'm very glad you're in here tonight, Peterkins, I've been meaning to give you a bell all day, but I just couldn't get round to it. I'm giving a little party tomorrow night, nothing special, you know, just a few chummies... oh yes, and one or two of the neighbours, Brian insists on inviting them, he's so boring about that sort of thing. Seven thirty, arrive whenever you like.

PETER: I can't come.

LOUISA: *(Enters with Campari soda puts it down in front of Fiona)* Campari and Soda. Happy Christmas Mrs Frobisher.

FIONA: And to you, Louisa. *(Louisa exits. Fiona turns to Peter)* What do you mean, you can't come?

PETER: Well, to tell the truth, I really don't feel like partying. I'd be a real pooper.

FIONA: You're not in Brian's class, darling. *(Drinks)* You've got to come. You and Rosie always came to my little Christmas soiree's.

PETER: Rosie isn't here any more.

FIONA: No Peter, she isn't, but she'd want you to come, I know she would. She certainly wouldn't want you lolling around at home on your own.

PETER: How on earth do you know what Rosie'd want? And in any case the real point is, I don't feel up to it.

FIONA: That's absolutely the weakest excuse I've ever heard in my life. Anyhow,

how do you know what you'll be feeling like tomorrow night.

PETER: Well I don't of course, but at the moment the thought of a party is the last thing I need. I'm feeling very low.

FIONA: You should try being married to Brian.

PETER: No thank you.

FIONA: Very wise. Why are you feeling low.

PETER: I was going to Gerald and Susan's for Christmas, it was all arranged. I was really looking forward to it, but they've got to go to New York on business.

FIONA: Lucky them. Of course you'd be very welcome to come to me...

PETER: *(Very Quickly)* No, no, I...

FIONA: Only we're going to Paris. I adore Paris. It's such a shame that Brian insists on coming.

PETER: Paris eh? So you won't be around for the festive season then? Good, good, I mean... it'll be lovely for you and Brian. Just the thing.

BRIAN: *(Offstage)* Fiona, I'm here. Hurry up I'm parked in a resticted area.

FIONA: *(Finishing drink. She gets up)* All right, all right. Finished all your little games then. *(Moves towards exit)* See you tomorrow evening, Peter darling.

PETER: I've already told you...

FIONA: Uncle Roger will be there, and besides I have a sneaky feeling that if you don't turn up, you could find yourself doing Reggie Thorven's part in the play, and it's much wordier than the one you're doing at the moment. See you darling. *(Blows a kiss)*

BRIAN: *(Offstage)* Come along Fiona!

FIONA: Oh, go and play with your apron. *(Exits)*.

(Lights down on pub. Lights up on Colin he is working at his word processor. Stops and looks at his watch. Picks up Telephone and dials number. Lights up on Rostrum. Telephone ringing as Peter enters from stage left. He picks up receiver.)

PETER: Hello, Peter Mason...

COLIN: Hello Peter, Colin here...

PETER: Colin? Oh Colin... yes... how are you?

COLIN: I'm baby sitting.

PETER: Oh... oh good heavens, you haven't got a problem have you? I don't know anything about babies, I mean, Jenny was one once, but I left it all to Rosie.

COLIN: *(Standing up)* It's all right Peter, your grandson is fast asleep. No, what I rang about was that Susan 'phoned earlier this evening and explained the situation, so I thought I'd get hold of you and proffer the festive board.

PETER: That's very kind of you Colin, but I couldn't possibly intrude. You've got quite enough on your plate what with the baby and your mother, no, no, I couldn't...

ROSIE: *(Upstage of Peter)* What did I say? When they were handing out faces, Peter certainly got two of them.

COLIN: Won't take no for an answer, Peter. Can't have you on your own for Christmas. I know Jenny would agree.

PETER: Doesn't she know?

COLIN: No, she's gone round to Aunty Phillipia, that's why I'm baby sitting.

PETER: Don't you think you ought to check with her?

ROSIE: That's got him thinking, you inviting him without asking Jenny. Nice one, Colin.

COLIN: No need for that at all. You're her Dad, she'll want you here.

PETER: Yes... well... that's very nice... eh thank you for thinking of me. I really do appreciate it. I was going to arrive at Gerald and Susan's round midday. Would it be all right if I came to you at the same time?

COLIN: No problem. Look forward to seeing you. Oh, Peter, would you mind bringing a couple of bottles of scotch? I don't want to run out and I know the vicar is looking in.

PETER: Leave it to me. I'll see you Christmas Eve then.

COLIN: Rightho Peter.

PETER: Colin?

COLIN: Yes?

PETER: Thank you. Bye. *(Puts telephone down).*

COLIN: *(Putting telephone down)* Don't count on a breakthrough, but we can always hope.

(Cut lights on Colin)

PETER: *(Rubbing his hands together gleefully)* Right then me hearties! Let's have a night cap! Aaarr! Jim Lad! *(Pours scotch).*

ROSIE: Thank you Colin. I know it wasn't easy, but you've done your bit... it's up to him now. Anyhow you've cheered him up. Ever since Susan 'phoned he's been going round the place with a face like a bucket of worms.

PETER:*(holding glass to Rosie's photograph)* Here's to us, who's like us, none thank God!

ROSIE: This is where my 'photo get's another slopping wet kiss.

PETER: Night Rosie, darling. Things are looking up at last. *(Kisses photograph and puts it on the table).*

ROSIE: The glass on that 'photo must be an absolute health hazard.

(Cut lights on Rostrum. Peter exits stage left. Rosie Stage right. Bring up lights on rostrum. Peter enters stage left carrying a holdall and suitcase. Puts them down and looks around)

PETER:"'twas the night before Christmas and all through the house nothing was stirring not even a mouse... " Now then, have I done everything? Cancelled the milk? Yes. Cancelled the papers? Yes. Mrs Johnson has a spare key in case of emergency. *(Looks at suitcase)* Shirts, socks, trousers,spare pair of shoes, knickers. *(Snaps his fingers)* What was it Colin asked me to bring?... Oh yes, couple of bottles of scotch. I'll get those at the off licence on the way out. Christmas presents? *(Looks at Holdall)* Yes, all packed. *(Looks at watch)* Just gone nine, plenty of time. *(Telephone rings. Crosses to it).*Hello, Peter Mason...

(Lights up on Colin. Colin sneezes loudly).

COLIN: Sorry.

PETER: Bless you.

COLIN: Peter, it's me, Colin. *(Coughs and sneezes).*

PETER: Hello there.

COLIN: This is awful Peter, but Jenny is in bed with flu, and I'm feeling like death warmed up.

PETER: You mean...

COLIN: There's a young epidemic up here. *(Coughs)* Mum came over last night and took Zech just to be on the safe side.

PETER: But its...

COLIN:I really am terribly sorry, but we'll have to cancel Christmas. *(No answer from Peter)* Peter...

PETER: Yes... still here.

COLIN: You understand, don't you?

PETER:... eh yes... yes of course... you can't help sickness.

COLIN: I must go Peter, I feel terrible.

PETER: Right... love to Jenny... take care... bye.

COLIN: Bye... Happy... *(Sneezes and coughs. Puts down telephone. Gets up and moves wearily to exit. Cut lights on Colin).*

PETER: *(Putting telephone down hard)* Would you Christmas bloody Eve it! What am I going to do. *(Kicks suitcase)* What am I going to do?

ROSIE: The stoical strain was never his strong point.

PETER: Oh my God! What am I going to eat? Where am I going to eat? I'll never book in any where now, not on Christmas eve morning. I'll have to go out shopping, and it'll be crowded. *(Looks around room)* Here... here's where I'll be this Christmas. If anyone wishes me the Compliments of the Season... I'll bloody kill them. *(Looks at telephone)* Oh Jenny, what did you have to go down with flu for, especially now.

ROSIE: Tremendous bedside manner. *(Sympathetically)* Poor old Peter.

PETER: Better go out and face the blasted hordes I suppose. It'll take ages.*(Puts hand on Rosie's photograph).* Tell me Rosie... why are you gone, and I'm still here? What's the point?

(Lights down on rostrum. Lights up on pub. Louisa enters and puts some beer mats on table and a Christmas candle. Peter enters carrying plastic carrier full of shopping.)

LOUISA: Hello Peter, Merry Christmas... here I thought you were...

PETER: *(Putting shopping down and sitting at table)* Long sad story.

LOUISA: Don't want to hear it.

PETER: Don't want to tell it.

LOUISA: Good. Arsenic or whisky?

PETER: Don't care.

LOUISA: *(moving towards exit)* Ah well, roll on half past one tomorrow afternoon.

PETER: Not open Christmas night?

LOUISA: No, thank the powers that be.

PETER: Oh... I thought... what does it matter?

LOUISA: *(Shouting to offstage)* All right, all right Clive, don't tap on the bar. I've told you about that before. *(To Peter)* I'll bring a whisky through. *(Exits)*.

PETER: Thanks. Happy Christmas. It's at times like this that I wished I smoked.

(Background Music and singing from other bar of 'God Rest Ye Merry Gentlemen'.)

PETER: Let nothing you dismay. Used to be my favourite carol... used to be... lots of things used to be.

(Anne enters Stage left. Stands looking at Peter for a moment.)

ANNE: Peter.

PETER: Anne... by all that's marvellous. *(Stands up and they shake hands)*.

ANNE:I've just come from your office. They told me about your daughter being ill. I'm so sorry.

PETER: Thank you. It's been a bit of an upset.

ANNE: Your secretary told me I'd probably find you in here. She said you'd looked in the office after you'd done your shopping. She seemed a bit concerned.

PETER: I'm okay. Nothing to worry about. What are you doing back here?

ANNE: Unexpected trip. The company I work for is thinking of taking over The Royal Sovereign, so I'm doing a sort of private recky. You know, the old business with pleasure routine.

PETER: Great. So you'll be here for a couple of days then? Oh, by the way, what'll you have?

ANNE: *(Sitting at table)* Gin and tonic please. No ice, no lemon.

PETER: *(Moving to exit)* Gin and tonic please, Louisa. No ice, no lemon.

LOUISA: *(Offstage)* Rightho Peter.

ANNE: *(As Peter moves back to table and sits)* I called at your office with a Christmas card, because I didn't know your home address. *(Opens handbag and gives Peter a Christmas card)*

PETER: Thank you, Anne. That's really thoughtful of you. Without being cliche, it's funny how little things mean a lot.

ANNE: It's nothing.*(Smiles broadly)* Peter, how about having dinner with me tonight? I know you're completely on your own. *(Chuckles)* Do you know, I've only seen you twice in the past five or six years, and on each of those occasions, I've asked you out to dinner. I hope you don't think I'm a scarlet woman.

PETER: I don't care what colour you are. I think you're very sweet and caring. *(Puts card on table)*

LOUISA: *(Entering with drinks)*One gin and tonic, one whisky.

PETER:(Giving Louisa a fiver)* Thanks Louisa. Put the change in the Children's Hospice Box.

LOUISA: Thank's very much, Peter. *(Exits)*

PETER: *(Picking up drink. To Anne)* Cheers. Merry Christmas, Anne.

ANNE: Cheers, Merry Christmas. *(Drinks)* Well, are you going to accept my invitation?

PETER: Yes please.

ANNE: Good. I don't think Christmas Eve is a good time to be on your own, do you?

PETER: Definitely not.*(Drinks)* But until you came in here I was resigned to it. What time shall I come?

ANNE: About seven, that okay with you?

PETER: Great.

ANNE: *(Glances at watch, gets up.)* Where's the 'phone Peter, there's a call I must make.

PETER: *(Pointing offstage)* Down the passage and just past the public bar.

ANNE: Thanks. *(Picks up handbag)* Shan't be long. *(Moves to exit. Looks back at Peter)* There's so much I want to talk to you about.*(Exits)*

PETER: *(Opening Christmas card)* Oh, Rosie, isn't that great. Look, 'To Peter sincere good wishes, and fondest memories of Rosie. And a kiss... I know it doesn't mean anything... we all put kisses... but it's nice... gives a sort of warm feeling. *(Puts card down. Looks at watch)* A Christmas. Present. I ought to get Anne a present didn't I? It would be the right thing to do, wouldn't it? I don't want her to think I'm... yes, yes I'm sure it's the right thing to do... Oh Lord, what can I get?

ROSIE: *(To the left of Peter)*Calm down and have a drink.

PETER: Steady on Peter. Calm down. *(Drinks)* I don't believe it... I actually feel excited.

ROSIE: Thank you, God. I don't know how you managed it, especially as it's a very busy time for you, but it's the nearest he's been to a human being for some considerable time. It suits him.

PETER: What shall I wear?

ROSIE: Anything but that Prince of Wales check. Makes him look like a walking chess board.

PETER: Eh... lets see. That Prince of Wales check suit is pretty dashing. No, no, Rosie didn't like it. The brown one? No, I'm not in a brown mood. I know, I'll wear the charcoal grey pin stripe.

ROSIE: What a splash of colour he's going to make.

PETER: *(Taking wallet out and a snap shot from it)* Love you Rosie. *(Kisses snapshot)* That's an extra kiss because... just because.

ROSIE: Hope that's not the one of me taken at Madge Tipper's wedding, my hair looked like a weeping willow in a thunder storm.

PETER: *(To photograph)* I wish you could tell me what to get for Anne.

ROSIE: Let's wait for the great unoriginal idea of all times.

PETER: Chocolates? Flowers? I took her flowers last time, and anyhow I can't face Mandy on a Christmas Eve.

ROSIE: Go into forward thinking Peter. It's the only way. Always remember that one minute you and I were US and the next minute you and I were YOU.

(Anne enters and stands looking at Peter who doesn't see her.)

PETER: *(To snapshot)* I'll always remember you Rosie. Whatever life has in store, you'll always be part of it. That's the real truth... the real hope. *(Puts snapshot away)*

(Anne moves slowly down and stands beside Peter.)

ROSIE: It's all right Peter. You can only love memories of me now, so don't waste the love that's still in you. Remember what I always believed. People are the only things that really matter in life... Anne is people. Don't forget what D.H. Lawrence said "The dead don't die. They look on and help".

(Lights fade slowly on Rosie, Peter and Anne. As this is happening we hear 'The smile you left behind' For a moment or two. The Curtain comes down.)

END

Performing Licence Applications

A performing licence for this play will be issued by "New Theatre Publications" subject to the following conditions.

Conditions

1. That the performance fee is paid in full on the date of application for a licence.
2. That the name of the Author(s) is/are clearly shown in any programme or publicity material.
3. That the Author(s) is/are entitled to receive two complimentary tickets to see his/her/their work in performance if they so wish.
4. That a copy of the play is purchased from New Theatre Publications for each named speaking part and a minimum of three copies purchased for backstage use.
5. That a copy of any review be forwarded to New Theatre Publications.
6. That the New Theatre Publications logo is clearly shown on any publicity material.

Fees payable for each public performance or public reading

Code	Type	Amateur under 300 seats	Amateur over 300 seats	Professional Production
A	One Act Play	£15	By Negotiation	M.T.A Rates
B	One Act Musical	£30	By Negotiation	M.T.A Rates
C	Full Length Play	£25	By Negotiation	M.T.A Rates
D	Full Length Musical	£50	By Negotiation	M.T.A Rates
E	Pantomime Script	£30	By Negotiation	M.T.A Rates
F	Pantomime + music	£60	By Negotiation	M.T.A Rates

To apply for a performing licence for any play please write to New Theatre Publications with the following details:-

1. **Name and address of theatre company.**
2. **Details of venue including seating capacity.**
3. **Dates of proposed performance or public reading.**
4. **Contact telephone number for Author's complimentary tickets.**

Widower's Way
A Drama
by Terry Harper

The play follows the adjustments required by Peter Mason after having become a widower approximately a year previous. Throughout the play we experience with him, his thoughts, actions and reactions, concerning his son and daughter-in-law, his daughter and her partner, his mother and various friends and acquaintances. Rosie, his dead wife features prominently in the play, observing, encouraging and criticising Peter's many changes of mood. Although the subject of bereavement is in no way funny, there are many scenes in the play that are amusing. The author hopes that audiences will see it as a "Heartwarming journey into hope".

"Thank you for supporting New Theatre Publications"
and
"The writing of New Theatre"

Please ask *your* local library to stock our plays!

You can visit our Web Site
at
Http://www.new-playwrights.demon.co.uk

Type: Drama . . . . . Length: Full-Length . . . . . Cast: 5M 10F
ISBN: 1 84094 085 9